TONY EVANS

SPEAKS OUT ON

FASTING

TONY EVANS
SPEAKS OUT ON
FASTING

MOODY PRESS
CHICAGO

Scripture quotations are taken from the *New American Standard Bible®*, ©
Copyright The Lockman Foundation 1960, 1962, 1963, 1968, 1971,
1972, 1973, 1975, 1977, 1995. Used by permission.

ISBN: 0-8024-4366-4

1 3 5 7 9 10 8 6 4 2

Printed in the United States of America

FASTING

THE IMPORTANCE OF FASTING

The story is told of a young lumberjack who had become quite proud of his speed at cutting down trees. He got to the point that he felt he was ready to challenge an older lumberjack, who was also known for his ability, to a tree-cutting contest.

So they began chopping. The younger man went at it with all his vigor. He chopped down one tree after another without stopping the whole day. He thought things looked pretty good for him because he noticed that the older lumberjack took about a fifteen-minute break every hour.

But at the end of the day, the older lumberjack had chopped down one-third more trees than the younger man. Somewhat miffed and puzzled, the younger man went to the old master of forestry and asked, "How in the world could you cut down more trees than me taking fifteen-minute breaks every hour?"

The wise older lumberjack looked at him and said, "Because when I stopped cutting, I took time to sharpen my ax."

That's a good parable of many Christians' spiritual lives. A lot of us chop away all the time, and then wonder why the trees aren't falling. We look at other people who don't seem to be working half as hard as we are, yet they seem to be making a lot more progress spiritually. Just maybe the difference is they have taken the time out to sharpen their axes.

That's what the spiritual discipline of fasting is all about—sharpening the "ax" of our inner person so we can achieve spiritual victory.

Most of us have heard a lot about prayer, but I wonder how much we have been taught about the importance and the purpose of fasting. Follow the subject through the Bible and you'll discover that it's everywhere. Fasting is not just an aside to the Christian life, but essential to the life that pleases God.

In fact, Jesus said that in His absence, fasting was to be a priority for His people. "The attendants of the bridegroom cannot mourn as long as the bridegroom is with them, can they? But the days will come when the bridegroom is taken away from them, and then they will fast" (Matthew 9:15).

Since you can't have a face-to-face conversation with Jesus today, fasting is a way you can make a special link with Him when you need a spiritual breakthrough in your life. I want to make four important points about fasting, and then look at fasting in three key areas: healing, protection, and ministry.

THE PRINCIPLE OF FASTING

Let's start with a definition. Fasting is the deliberate abstinence from some form of physical gratification, for a period of time, in order to achieve a greater spiritual goal.

Fasting usually involves setting aside food, although we can fast from any physical appetite, including sex within marriage (1 Corinthians 7:5). A lot of Christians need to fast from the hours they spend watching television or surfing the Internet. The idea is to devote the time we would ordinarily spend on these activities to prayer and waiting before the Lord. Fasting calls us to renounce the natural in order to invoke the supernatural. When you fast, you say no to yourself so you can hear yes from God in a time of need or crisis.

As I said earlier, fasting is a major principle throughout the Bible. People in Scripture often fasted in situations that demanded a spiritual breakthrough. Fasting is an appropriate response to physical or emotional needs, difficult circumstances or relationships, challenges in ministry (as we will see later), or times we need specific direction.

In Zechariah 7:5–6, the Lord said, "When you fasted and mourned in the fifth and seventh months these seventy years, was it actually for Me that you fasted? When you eat and drink, do you not eat for yourselves and do you not drink for yourselves?"

Even though the fasts God referred to here would have been unnecessary if His people had repented, these verses still give us an important principle about fasting. When we eat, we eat for ourselves, with nothing more than our own satisfaction in mind. But when we fast, we should do so with God in mind, for His pleasure.

When I sit down before the "gospel bird," my fried chicken, after church on Sunday, I don't pick up a leg or thigh and wonder what the associate pastor at our church is doing. I know what he's doing—the same thing I'm doing!

When I'm hungry, my stomach cries out, "Feed me." I answer, "I am your obedient servant. Whatever you say, I will do."

We become servants to the cry of our flesh to receive food. We eat for ourselves. But when we fast, God says, "This is for Me." Just as food satisfies us, fasting satisfies God because we are saying to Him, "The cry of my soul for You is greater than the cry of my stomach for food or anything else." That's why fasting gets God's attention like nothing else.

To understand the impact of fasting you need to understand the reason behind it. God created Adam out of the dust from the ground. The elements in our bodies are only worth a few dollars on the open market.

It wasn't until God breathed into Adam's nostrils the breath of life that he became "a living being" (Genesis 2:7). Your ultimate value is not in your body, but in your soul. It's the nonmaterial part of us that is in God's image, not our bodies.

What do we do so often? We feed the body, even overstuff it, while starving the soul. But when we fast, we give the soul a higher priority than the body. We are asking God to feed our souls.

This is the principle of fasting. The question is, Are you willing to give up your steak and potatoes to gain spiritual riches? Are you willing to sacrifice that which gratifies the flesh in order to make an investment in that which builds up the spirit?

Some people in business will go all day without stopping to eat if they're trying to close a major deal. In other words, the value of the deal overrides the value of a meal. God is saying the same thing holds true in the spiritual life. Fasting teaches us to give up a craving of the body because we have a deeper need of the soul.

THE PURPOSE OF FASTING

Let's talk about the why of fasting. According to Isaiah 58:4, the purpose of fasting is "to make your voice heard on high." When we fast with the proper motivation, our voice is heard in heaven. That is, we come into God's presence in a powerful way.

So much of our time with God is spent on the run. We run before Him, throw out a few requests, and move on. But the nature of fasting is such that it demands concentrated effort and time to come into God's presence.

Think about the effort we make to eat when we're hungry. Most of us will make a way where there is no way when it's mealtime. We'll change our route to hit the drive-through window at the fast-food restaurant. We'll make a sandwich out of stuff in the refrigerator that is "unsandwichable."

Why? Because we are desperate to satisfy our hunger. But when you fast, you are desperate to satisfy a need in your soul. You are desperate to make your voice heard on high.

In Isaiah 58:5, the Lord says fasting is "a day for a man to humble himself." It is a humbling experience to say no to something you crave, to bow low before God and admit there is a need in your life. Fasting demands humility, and humility means self-denial.

Something unique happens when we fast. God sharpens our spiritual focus so we can see things more clearly. Jesus fasted for forty days before facing the devil (Matthew 4:1–11). And when Satan tempted Him to make bread out of the stones, Jesus said, "Man shall not live on bread alone, but on every word that proceeds out of the mouth of God" (v. 4).

One purpose of fasting is to show you how well you are doing with your inner person. Some people spend all of their time making their outer person beautiful, while their inner person is downright ugly. In fact, the uglier the inner person, the more some people spend trying to camouflage it.

We are spiritual beings, and fasting helps us to acknowledge and feed our spiritual nature. It says that there is more to me than what you see.

In 1 Thessalonians 5:23, Paul prayed that his readers would be sanctified and preserved in their "spirit and soul and body." Paul's order here is purposeful. We are not made up of body, soul, and spirit, but spirit, soul, and body. We are created to live from the inside out, not from the outside in.

You say, "Why is that important?" Because if you look at yourself as a body that happens to house a soul and a spirit, you will live for your body first. But if you understand that you are spirit at the core of your being, you will live for the spirit.

Your spirit is the part of you that enables you to communicate with God. It gives you God-awareness. Your soul enables you to communicate with yourself. It gives you self-awareness. Your body enables you to communicate with your environment. It gives you other-awareness.

We need to live from our spirit out to our bodies. The reason so many people have messed-up bodies is because they have messed-up souls. And the reason they have messed-up souls is because their spirits are not under the control of the Holy Spirit. If we want to really live, the spirit or the inner person must be set free. Our spirits must be cracked open to release the Spirit's life, and fasting helps us do this.

I liken this process to the popping of popcorn. You can't eat unpopped popcorn because the shell is too hard. It will break your teeth.

But every kernel of popcorn has moisture in the center. When you put the corn in the microwave, the microwave heats up the moisture, which becomes steam, and the steam pushes against the shell.

All of a sudden you hear a pop, followed by many more as the shells of the popcorn kernels are cracked open to reveal the edible part of the corn. You wouldn't think that tiny shell could hold all of that stuff, because the shell is suppressing what's on the inside. But the environment of the microwave oven breaks open the shell to bring out what's inside.

When you come to God in the environment of fasting, He heats up your spirit, which inflames your soul, which then breaks through your body and results in righteous living. That's a great result, but it only happens when you come into God's presence and bow before Him in humility and allow Him to break you. To be broken means to be stripped of your self-sufficiency.

But too often, our problem is that we aren't ready for God to do that. We make all kinds of resolutions and promises, which are really just ways of saying to God, "I can do this myself." But if we could do it, we would have already done it.

Fasting puts us on the path of humility.

What God wants to hear is, "Lord, I can't do this. I've tried everything I know and I can't get rid of these cigarettes. I can't break my lust for pornography. I can't quit these drugs. I am ruined and broken. Lord, I throw my inability and my failure at Your feet."

God says, "Now I can do something."

You see, when we fail to humble ourselves before God, what we wind up doing is trying to live the Christian life in our own power. We call on our flesh to help us defeat the flesh—which is a contradiction in terms. What we need is to get the flesh out of the way, to set it aside in order to focus on the spirit. Fasting is a tangible way of demonstrating to God that we are setting aside the flesh in order to deal with the spirit.

More than that, fasting is also a way of prostrating ourselves before God. In the Bible, when people were broken before the Lord they often fell on their faces. They put ashes on their heads and tore their clothes as a way of saying, "Lord, I can't do anything. I am at the end of my rope."

God wants us to reach that point so He can demonstrate His power and get all the glory, which He deserves. The apostle James says those who humble themselves before God will be lifted up (James 4:10). As we have said, fasting puts us on the path of humility.

What can a man and woman do to help heal their marriage if they are having problems? Paul says a married couple can agree to enter a sexual fast (1 Corinthians 7:5) if they have something urgent to pray about. They can use the time they would normally use being intimate to pray, just as a person who is fasting from food uses his mealtime to pray rather than eat.

I'm confident that most Christian couples who have

problems in their marriages have never considered a sexual fast, during which they throw themselves on the mercy of God to deal with the problems in their marriage. If some couples would practice sexual fasting and prayer before heading downtown to the divorce judge, we might have fewer divorces in the church. Note that Paul does not command this particular kind of fast, and this kind of decision is highly individual to each couple. The command in this verse is to come together sexually, with the fast as the temporary exception. It should be entered into only by mutual agreement and perhaps with counsel in the case of a troubled marriage.

There would also be fewer problems with drugs and other addictions if more people came to the end of themselves and fell on their faces before God in fasting and prayer.

THE PRACTICE OF FASTING

What does a person do who wants to practice fasting?

The details of a fast are really up to the individual in terms of the length and nature of the fast. That needs to be a matter of conviction between you and God.

David said he put on sackcloth during a fast (Psalm 69:11). We don't usually practice the outward signs of fasting today. In fact, Jesus told us not to make it obvi- ous to others that we are fasting (Matthew 6:16–18).

But there are some common elements to the fasts we read about in Scripture. One is the attitude of humility before the Lord we talked about earlier. For people in Scripture, putting on sackcloth and ashes was a sign of that humility.

Another common element in the practice of fasting is prayer. Listen to the prayer David offered during his fast:

> My prayer is to You, O Lord, at an acceptable time; O God, in the greatness of Your lovingkindness, answer me with Your saving truth. Deliver me from the mire and do not let me sink; may I be delivered from my foes and from the deep waters. May the flood of water not overflow me nor the deep swallow me up, nor the pit shut its mouth on me. (Psalm 69:13–15)

Ever felt like you were sinking in the mire? Or that circumstances were flooding in on you? When that's happening, you need to hear from God. David came before God in humility and fasting and prayer.

God told His people through the prophet Joel, "Return to Me with all your heart, and with fasting, weeping and mourning; and rend your heart and not your garments" (Joel 2:12–13a). Fasting is a serious time of coming before God.

But it is also a time of praise. Joel went on to say, "[The Lord] is gracious and compassionate, slow to anger, abounding in lovingkindness and relenting of evil. Who knows whether He will not turn and relent and leave a blessing behind Him?" (vv. 13b–14). Then the prophet said, "Consecrate a fast" (v. 15).

The question in fasting is, How badly do you want an answer? How much do you want deliverance from that destructive habit? How badly do you want to save your marriage? Do you want it enough to give up food or some other gratification? Then come before God with prayer and praise in fasting.

You may feel like giving up on a problem, but if you haven't fasted over it yet, you haven't done everything you can do. You have one more option—to throw yourself on the mercy of God in humility while giving up a craving of the flesh for a greater need of the spirit.

Let me make a suggestion that will help you as you practice fasting. Get a notebook and draw a line down the middle of the page. On one side write down what you want God to do—and be specific. "I need healing in this part of my body." "I want to win my mother to Christ." "I want to be delivered from the curse of pornography."

Then lay these needs before the Lord as you fast and pray. Say to the Lord what Jacob said: "I will not let you go unless you bless me" (Genesis 32:26). Then as God answers prayer, record the answer on the opposite side of the page.

THE PAYOFF FOR FASTING

What can we expect God to do when we fast? What's the spiritual payoff for fasting?

Let's go back to Isaiah 58, a great passage on fasting. The Lord asks, "Is this not the fast which I choose, to loosen the bonds of wickedness, to undo the bands of the yoke, and to let the oppressed go free and break every yoke?" (v. 6).

Some of us are living with spiritual handcuffs on, trying to praise the Lord when we can't even raise our hands because we are handcuffed. When we walk out of church, we walk right back into bondage because Satan has us in handcuffs. He knows that when we wake up in the morning, all he has to do is bring that thought across our minds, and he has us.

But when we fast, God says He will break the chains and the yoke of the addictions and problems that we can't break ourselves and that no one else can break for us. God says if we haven't fasted yet, we haven't been to the right program. God *is* the program.

Then in Isaiah 58:7, the Lord continued by saying, "Is [this fast] not to divide your bread with the hungry and bring the homeless poor into the house; when you see the naked, to cover him; and not to hide yourself from your own flesh?"

Now this is deep. You can't divide your bread with the hungry unless you have bread to divide. You can't bring the homeless into the house unless you have a house. You can't clothe the naked unless you have clothing to give them.

When you are willing to humble yourself before God and fast, He can bless your business so that you have bread to share. He can enlarge your home so that you can use it to minister to others. But please notice that God is only interested in blessing you if you are going to be a conduit of His blessing to others.

God doesn't mind blessing you as long as He can use you. But if God blesses you and then even He can't use your stuff and it's never available to His kingdom, God says that is not the kind of fast He is interested in. God wants to change your circumstances so you can help others and you won't have to "hide yourself" from your family or anyone else because something is wrong.

Now look at Isaiah 58:8. God says through the prophet, "Then your light will break out like the dawn." After you have fasted and your voice has been heard on high, then the butterfly will emerge from the cocoon.

You see, we have been given all the spiritual resources of God in Jesus Christ. These blessings are located "in the heavenly places," which is where we have been seated by virtue of our position in Christ (Ephesians 1:3; 2:6).

But some believers who are seated in the heavenly places with Christ don't even know where the chair is. They are positioned next to Christ Himself, but they don't even know where in the world that is.

Why is that? Because the flesh is so dominant sometimes. What we need to do is weaken the flesh so the Holy Spirit can break through.

One way to weaken the hold the flesh has on us is through fasting. When you starve the flesh, it gets weak. If you are going to fast more than one meal, you are going to feel weak. That's OK, because now the flesh can't buck up like it used to. When you keep the flesh strong, it can rear its head and say, "I run this show. I'm in charge here. Let's eat."

But once the flesh starts to get weak, we become strong in the Lord's strength. Paul said he was strongest spiritually in his physical weakness (2 Corinthians 12:10).

Notice also in Isaiah 58 that God said, "The glory of the Lord will be your rear guard" (v. 8c). The enemy can't sneak up on you when God is covering your back.

All of this is the payoff for fasting. The bottom line is this: "You will call, and the Lord will answer; you will cry, and He will say, 'Here I am'" (Isaiah 58:9).

You may say, "But I've been calling to God all this time." Are you calling to Him with the fast? Remember, fasting makes your voice heard on high. God wants to be treated seriously.

Before we look at some specific situations in which fasting is called for, let me tell you what you can expect when you start taking seriously the discipline of fasting.

Let me explain it by way of an illustration. Since about 1937, airplanes have been pressurized so they can fly above the clouds. Before then, they had to fly low so they could stay in the atmosphere.

As soon as you start fasting and praying, Satan and his demons are going to line up at cloud level. And they are going to try to keep you below the clouds so you don't fly high and reach the throne of God.

But if you fast and throw yourself on the mercy of God, you are going to break through the clouds because God will "pressurize" your soul so you can breathe up there in the heavenly places where God's blessings and power are.

So don't let Satan keep you on the ground. It is time to fly. It is time to get the flesh under control so you are not under its control.

FASTING FOR HEALING

Now that we have laid a biblical foundation for the discipline of fasting, let's see how it relates to three key areas of life. The first is healing.

This issue is usually referred to as divine healing, and that's a good term because God is the source of all healing, whether He uses intermediate means such as medical science or heals directly. Healing is not limited to physical healing, but can go beyond that to emotional and spiritual healing.

It is unfortunate today that so much teaching on the subject of healing has departed far from what God had in mind in Scripture. For example, a lot of people today are seeking what I call "cosmetic healing."

This kind of healing is sort of like cosmetic surgery, which is often done simply to enhance people's appearance and satisfy their vanity. More often than not, cosmetic surgery is performed to satisfy a person's wants regardless of that person's needs.

That's different than reconstructive plastic surgery. This is plastic surgery done to take care of a serious need, such as when a person is severely burned or needs to have birth defects repaired.

God is not interested in simply being your cosmetic Healer to make you look better. But if you're interested in reconstruction, He can deal with you. One thing we'll learn about fasting for healing is that God has a bigger agenda than our personal satisfaction or comfort.

I want to give some principles from God's Word that I hope will help you find balance between the two extremes on divine healing: the extreme that makes healing an end in itself and promises full healing to everyone, and the extreme that relegates healing and other miracles to yesteryear.

Fasting for Healing Is Within God's Will

The first principle I want us to see is that fasting for healing is well within the scope of God's will.

Some people teach that physical health is always God's will for all of His people at all times. These folk have a hard time explaining Paul's physical malady, however (2 Corinthians 12:1–10). The apostle pleaded with God to take it away, but the answer was, "My grace is sufficient for you" (v. 9).

This doesn't mean God is opposed to our health. John wrote to Gaius in 3 John 2, "I pray that in all respects you may prosper and be in good health, just as your soul prospers." But please notice John's emphasis on Gaius's spiritual health. We can't let our passion for physical well-being override our passion for spiritual well-being.

But having said that, God is still *Jehovah Rapha,* "the Lord . . . your healer" (Exodus 15:26). God heals in two ways. He may heal preventively, taking care of a problem before we even know something is wrong. God has designed the human body in such a way that it can heal itself.

God also heals curatively, after an illness has come. He may work through the body's own healing system or through the intervention of the medical profession. And on occasion, God simply chooses to reach out His sovereign hand and heal a person instantly without any secondary agent.

We are going to see several occasions in Scripture where people fasted for healing, either their own or someone else's. But fasting is not designed to replace medicine. Even Jesus said sick people need a physician (Luke 5:31).

We said earlier that fasting is giving up a craving of the body, or some other need, because of a greater need of the spirit. Things such as food, money, and health are gifts from God, but when you fast you forego the gift in order to get in touch with the Giver. Fasting elevates the Giver over the gift.

So when we fast for healing we are telling God we recognize that He sits above medical science. We can use the skills of doctors and the marvels of medicine, but God must be our source of trust. It is the Lord who heals us.

In 2 Chronicles 16 there is a dramatic example of someone who failed to recognize this fact. King Asa of Judah became very ill with a disease in his feet. But the Bible says, "Even in his disease [Asa] did not seek the Lord, but the physicians. So Asa slept with his fathers" (vv. 12–13).

You need to read those verses together to get the impact. King Asa's illness may have been an infection in his feet that eventually poisoned his whole body. The text doesn't say specifically whether God would have healed him, but it does say that Asa refused to seek the Lord and died.

Some of God's people may be experiencing health problems at a level they don't need to experience because they have looked to the doctors but haven't looked to the Lord in prayer and fasting. That would be tragic, because fasting for healing is within God's will for us.

Fasting for Healing Promotes God's Program

A second principle of fasting for healing is that when you do so, make sure you are promoting God's program. Let me show you what I mean through the biblical story of Hannah.

Hannah was a godly woman who was greatly loved by her husband, Elkanah. But she was barren because "the Lord had closed her womb" (1 Samuel 1:5). Hannah's inability to bear children was a form of illness, but it was an illness sent by God for His purposes. So anybody who tells you that if you're sick you're out of God's will doesn't understand who God is or how He works.

Worse than Hannah's barrenness was that Elkanah's other wife, Peninnah, constantly ridiculed Hannah for her inability to conceive (vv. 6–7). Hannah felt the pain of this because in Israel the failure to have children was considered a curse, a judgment, from God.

Hannah's physical condition, and her desire to have a child, left her in deep emotional and spiritual distress. She was in such turmoil of heart that she refused to eat (vv. 7–8), entering a fast as she sought the Lord for a remedy to her problem.

It was in this period of fasting and prayer that Hannah made a vow to the Lord (1 Samuel 1:11). If God would give her a son, she would give him back to the Lord to serve the Lord "all the days of his life."

Notice that Hannah did not simply ask God to grant her request so she could be happy and remove the stigma from her life. Her prayer for the healing of her infertility is for God's greater glory. She wants a son whose life will further God's program and embellish His kingdom.

There are folk on a hospital bed who pray, "Lord, if You will raise me up, I'll serve You for the rest of my life." God raised them up, but He hasn't seen them since. When these people got their strength back, God got less of them, not more of them.

Fasting sets us on the pursuit of God's grace.

But that wasn't the case with Hannah. After her intense time of prayer at the temple, God healed her womb and enabled her to conceive, and Hannah gave birth to Samuel (1 Samuel 1:19–20). And then when the time came, Hannah fulfilled her promise to God by bringing Samuel to Eli the priest at the temple (vv. 24–25). Samuel went on to become a great prophet and judge in Israel.

Samuel was a miracle baby—but Hannah received a miracle because she had God's greater program in view. The Bible says, "The Lord remembered her" (v. 19), but not because God had forgotten about Hannah. Instead, He remembered her by responding to the intensity of her commitment, which was demonstrated by fasting and prayer.

Fasting for Healing Pursues God's Grace

Here's a third principle we need to know about the issue of fasting for healing. This kind of fasting sets us on the pursuit of God's grace. We're going to look at an example of this in 2 Samuel 12.

This is the story of what happened after King David committed adultery with Bathsheba and then had her husband, Uriah, killed in battle. The baby that resulted from this adulterous relationship became sick, and David fasted and prayed for the baby's healing.

Although it's not always the case, sin can certainly be one reason for sickness. Just ask the Corinthians. Paul told them that some of the people in their assembly were eating the Lord's Supper "in an unworthy manner" and were therefore "guilty of the body and the blood of the Lord" (1 Corinthians 11:27).

This was the reason, Paul wrote, that "many among you are weak and sick, and a number sleep" (v. 30). Some of these believers had actually died as a result of God's judgment. One of the ways God addresses the rebellion of His children is through sickness (see Deuteronomy 28:22).

When sin is the cause of illness, repentance and forgiveness are in order. We'll see later that the apostle James instructed a sick person to confess any known sin and said that if the sin was the reason for the illness, God would bring relief. Jesus said to a crippled man, "Your sins are forgiven" (Mark 2:5). Then He told the man to take up his bed and walk.

David's situation was a little unusual in that while he wasn't the sick person, his sin was the cause of the problem. There is no doubt that this was God's discipline, because we read, "The Lord struck the child that Uriah's widow bore to David, so that he was very sick" (2 Samuel 12:15).

When David learned his baby boy was sick, the king fell prostrate before the Lord. "David therefore inquired of God for the child; and David fasted and went and lay all night on the ground" (v. 16). According to verse 18, David fasted and prayed on his face before God for a week.

David threw himself on God's grace because he knew he had no other grounds for approaching God. The penalty for adultery and murder in Israel was death. David himself said his fast was a means of seeking God's grace. "While the child was still alive, I fasted and wept; for I said, 'Who knows, the Lord may be gracious to me, that the child may live'" (v. 22).

Now we know that David's child died despite his week of fasting and prayer. So was David's fast a failure? Did he receive God's grace?

Before we answer these questions, we need to remember that fasting is not a magic wand we wave before God to get what we want. David fasted for the right reasons. He was pursuing God's grace. He was repentant for the sins of adultery and murder.

But David's fast did not undo the fact that Bathsheba had been violated and Uriah was dead. David still had to pay the consequences of his sin, even though God had forgiven him (2 Samuel 12:13–14). David lost his son, but he did receive God's healing grace. God was gracious to David in at least two ways.

First, after the baby's death David ended his fast, worshiped the Lord, and then went home and ate (v. 20). In other words, even though God did not change the situation and heal David's child, God restored David's life to him. He gave David the grace to go on in spite of the pain and the loss he felt.

I am not here to tell you that every time you fast, God is going to do what you want when you want it. But I am here to tell you God is gracious even if He doesn't change the situation.

Notice the second way God showed David His grace.

David comforted His wife Bathsheba, and went in to her and lay with her; and she gave birth to a son, and he named him Solomon. Now the Lord loved him and sent word through Nathan the prophet, and he named him Jedidiah for the Lord's sake. (2 Samuel 12:24–25)

Jedidiah means "beloved of the Lord." God was saying to David, "I am giving your new son My name to remind you that My grace has now come into this relationship."

Many believers can testify that when they fasted for God's healing grace in a physical or emotional or relational need, God was indeed gracious to them even when the situation itself did not change. It's wonderful when God heals, but even when He chooses not to do so His grace is still abundant. Fasting is a powerful way of seeking God's grace.

Fasting for Healing Honors God's Word

The story of the prophet Daniel teaches us another important principle concerning fasting. Daniel and his three friends didn't need healing in terms of deliverance from a disease, but they did need for God to do a special work in their bodies.

The issue came up when Daniel and his friends were taken from Jerusalem to Babylon as captives. King Nebuchadnezzar turned these Hebrew boys over to his assistants to prepare them for service in his court.

This preparation included eating the king's "choice food" (Daniel 1:5), which Daniel refused to eat (v. 8). Why? Because doing so would cause him to violate God's law by eating food that the law prohibited or that had been defiled by being part of pagan rituals.

So Daniel and his three friends entered a partial fast. They didn't fast from food altogether, just from the king's defiled food and wine. Daniel asked the king's assistant to feed them vegetables and water for ten days, and then test them (vv. 12–13).

Daniel was taking a risk, because if the plan failed, not only the king's assistant, but all of them, could have been put to death for displeasing King Nebuchadnezzar. But Daniel was determined to honor God's Word as revealed in His law, and his fast was part of that commitment. Daniel was trusting God to honor him in turn. Faith always needs to be linked to fasting.

God did honor Daniel's commitment. "At the end of ten days their appearance seemed better and they were fatter than all the youths who had been eating the king's choice food" (Daniel 1:15).

God also gave them a bonus for honoring Him: "As for these four youths, God gave them knowledge and intelligence in every branch of literature and wisdom; Daniel even understood all kinds of visions and dreams" (v. 17).

For Daniel, the issue was clear. He knew what God's Word taught concerning clean and defiled food, so his decision wasn't hard to make. He knew that to eat less and obey God was better than to eat more and disobey God. So he fasted from the king's food, trusting God to bring about the desired physical result.

Fasting for Healing Develops God's People

One of the most familiar stories in the Bible is the conversion of the apostle Paul, who saw a vision of Jesus Christ and was converted on the road to Damascus (Acts 9:1–8). I want to look at this account as we consider a final principle of fasting for healing.

When Paul arrived in Damascus as a brand-new Christian, he was blind for three days, and also "neither ate nor drank" (Acts 9:9). This former persecutor of the church needed to be humbled, and now he was completely dependent on God. Not only was Paul blind, but he didn't yet know what God wanted him to do (see v. 6). So he began fasting as he sought God's direction for the future—and, I'm sure, for healing from his blindness.

It's obvious here that fasting was an important part of Paul's spiritual development. One of the reasons God allows illness in our lives is that when we are on our backs, the only place we can look is up. God will allow believers to get sick as a trial in order to develop them spiritually.

God had a big plan for Paul, so he had to prepare Paul in a big way by testing him through a big problem. "He is a chosen instrument of Mine, to bear My name before the Gentiles and kings and the sons of Israel" (v. 15). That ministry would demand that Paul be able to endure suffering and hardship.

If God has given you a big problem, look to Him because He's up to something big in your life. Some of the best times you can have with God are when you're not feeling well, because then you don't want to be bothered with anything else but Him. Fasting for healing, and for God's will in your sickness, is one way God can prepare you to be used by Him in a greater way.

Before we move on, I need to answer an important question about healing. What should God's people do to seek His healing today? According to James 5:14, "Is anyone among you sick? Then he must call for the elders of the church and they are to pray over him, anointing him with oil in the name of the Lord."

The word *sick* here means "weak," which could mean a physical, psychological, emotional, or spiritual weakness. The sick person must take the initiative, which shows that he or she really wants God to intervene in the situation.

The elders are to "pray over [the sick one], anointing him with oil in the name of the Lord" (v. 14). In biblical days, oil was used both as a medicine and for grooming—refreshment and restoration, in other words. This is the anointing James was referring to.

The elders were to anoint the sick or weak person with oil as a symbol of the refreshment and restoration that God would bring into the person's life in fulfillment of the following promise: "And the prayer offered in faith will restore the one who is sick, and the Lord will raise him up" (v. 15).

If an illness is the direct result of sin, and if the sin is confessed and removed, then the sick person can expect to be restored to health. That's why James says, "If he has committed sins, they will be forgiven him" (v. 15b). But what about believers who are physically sick, or weak and weary in some other way, such as emotionally or spiritually? The promise is that if they will call for the elders, they will be restored.

Why the anointing with oil by the elders? Because they are the formal representatives of the church, and it is the church's job to act on Christ's behalf. The elders may not be the means of your healing, but they can make sure the church brings you the restoration and refreshment that Jesus has for you. He wants you to feel His encouraging, grooming touch.

Let me emphasize again, James 5 is not saying that everyone will be healed. But it does promise that everyone will be restored, for the church is God's community of restoration.

FASTING FOR PROTECTION

One of my favorite stories growing up was "The Three Little Pigs." I was always intrigued by the big bad wolf's ability to simply blow down the first two pigs' houses.

All of the pigs' houses had been built to protect them from the big bad wolf, who sought their destruction. But the first two pigs discovered that if you don't use the right protective materials, the wolf cannot be kept out. Only the third pig, who built his house of brick, was protected from the enemy.

We need protection today as desperately as the three little pigs, for we face a powerful enemy who is bent on coming into our homes and devouring us and our families. We need protection from Satan and his emissaries. That's why Jesus taught us to pray, "Deliver us from evil" (Matthew 6:13). That is a prayer for God's protection.

There are a number of reasons we need to pray for protection. One is the fact that Satan seeks our destruction. His purpose is "to steal and kill and destroy" (John 10:10). He would love nothing better than to render us ineffective in God's kingdom and then take us out.

We also need protection from evil people who are being used by Satan to carry out his agenda. Now don't misunderstand. People themselves are not the enemy. The devil behind the people energizing them to do evil is the enemy. But we need protection from the attitudes and actions of people who seek our demise and the demise of God's kingdom work.

We need to pray for God's protection every day. But sometimes we also need to fast for God's protection. In the Bible, we often find people fasting when they were surrounded by their enemies, under a dire threat of destruction, facing Satan and his demonic realm, and overcome by fear.

I don't have the space to look at all of the passages that describe God's people fasting and praying for protection, but I suggest it as a great study for you to do with your Bible and a concordance. Here I want to consider the story of Queen Esther, which tells of a time when God's people sought Him through fasting and presumably also through prayer in a time of terrible crisis.

Before we turn to Esther, let me ask an important question that you may be asking right now, and suggest an answer. How do you know when it's time for you to fast for God's protection?

The sign that you need to go deeper with God on

this is when you're dominated by fear. When fear controls you, when something in your life seems even bigger than God's ability to protect you, this is an indication it's time for you to seek God by fasting.

Fasting for Protection Deals with Our Fear

Let me briefly set the context for our study of Esther. She was the beautiful young Jewish exile in the kingdom of Persia who was chosen by King Ahasuerus to become queen. Esther became the king's favorite, but the key to the plot is that no one in the Persian court knew Esther was a Jew.

Esther had an older Jewish relative named Mordecai, who served as her guardian in Persia. While Esther was finding favor with the king, Mordecai fell into disfavor with Haman, the king's top adviser. Haman was a cruel man who came to hate Mordecai bitterly when the latter refused to bow down to Haman like everyone else did. To bow to Haman would have been a violation of God's law, and Mordecai refused to do it.

Haman's hatred was so intense that he wasn't content just to kill Mordecai (Esther 3:6). Haman convinced King Ahasuerus that the whole Jewish race was made up of disloyal troublemakers who were bad news for his kingdom. So at Haman's prompting, the king signed an edict calling for the slaughter of all Jews in Persia on a given day. That's how evil is. Satan doesn't want just you. He wants your whole family.

Talk about evil people manipulated by Satan. The devil was clever, because he knew Persian law could never be changed once it had been enacted. In other words, there was no human way to undo Haman's decree. Haman became Satan's tool to achieve his number one goal, the total destruction of God's people.

So all the Jews in Persia were now under a death sentence, and this is where we pick up the story. Mordecai went into mourning, and Esther sent a servant to find out why. Mordecai sent back a copy of the king's edict with the message, "You've got to do something, girl. Go to the king and plead for the lives of your people. You're a Jew, and you'll die too if Haman's edict is carried out."

God is never backed into a corner.

All of this leads to the climactic passage in Esther 4 that we want to examine. When Esther got the bad news, she sent a message back to Mordecai, which I'll summarize.

"Mordecai, anyone who goes in to the king without being called will be put to death unless the king decides otherwise. If I go to the king now to appeal for the Jews, I'll be killed, because he hasn't called for me for the past thirty days" (see Esther 4:11).

Esther was saying, "Mordecai, I know I'm a Jew, and I know you used to be my guardian and I love you and all of that. But you can't expect me to risk my life for you. If I go in to see Ahasuerus, I'm a dead queen."

Esther was afraid, and for good reason. She was gripped with fear because she knew the rules of the house, and she didn't want to die. As far as she could see, there was no one to protect her from the king's wrath.

But the Jews in Persia also needed protection. So Mordecai sent this word back to Esther:

> Do not imagine that you in the king's palace can escape any more than all the Jews. For if you remain silent at this time, relief and deliverance will arise for the Jews from another place and you and your father's house will perish. And who knows whether you have not attained royalty for such a time as this? (Esther 4:13–14)

Notice what Mordecai said. He was confident that if Esther didn't come through, God would use someone else to deliver His people.

Mordecai's great statement teaches us two principles we need to understand when it comes to the matter of God's protection. First, God always provides a ram in the bush, the way He provided for Abraham (see Genesis 22:13). When you need God's protection, He has ways of protecting you that you may know nothing about. God is never backed into a corner.

Here's a second principle we learn from Mordecai. We need to be part of the solution. Even when we're in the grip of fear and things look bad, we can't just hide under the table and refuse to be used by God. If we do that, He will bypass us and use someone else.

Mordecai wanted Esther to understand that she had not been chosen queen just because she was so pretty that Ahasuerus couldn't take his eyes off her. God had made her the queen "for such a time as this," for this time when His people were being threatened with annihilation.

Esther needed to understand the theology of this situation. That is, she needed to see things from God's perspective. So Mordecai gave her a theological response that showed her the real deal. By the way, make sure you have a Mordecai in your life—somebody who will hold you responsible for doing what is right.

Fasting for Protection Activates God's Power

Esther was afraid, but she also saw the need the Jews had for protection from Haman.

So Esther addressed her fear by sending this message back to Mordecai:

> Go, assemble all the Jews who are found in Susa, and fast for me; do not eat or drink for three days, night or day. I and my maidens also will fast in the same way. And thus I will go in to the king, which is not according to the law; and if I perish, I perish. (Esther 4:16)

At this point, Esther was more afraid of King Ahasuerus than she was of God. That may be your situation today. You may be more afraid of your boss or someone else, or more intimidated by your circumstance, than you are confident in God's ability to protect you.

You must turn that fear into faith, and one way to do that is by fasting and prayer.

The fast Esther called for was a major event, since it involved her and Mordecai and all the Jews in the Persian capital of Susa. Her decision to fast also helped Esther get a God-oriented perspective on her situation.

When Esther said, "If I perish, I perish," she wasn't being fatalistic. She was saying, "God is sovereign, and while I am going to fast for protection, the final outcome is His."

God taught me that lesson in an unforgettable way during my college days. I used to go out almost every Friday and preach on the street corner in Atlanta. People would gather on the corner to catch the bus, so I'd have a ready congregation.

One day while I was preaching, a man kept interrupting me. The Word was irritating him, and he told me if I didn't stop preaching I'd never be able to preach again. Then he put his hand inside his coat.

I didn't know what that man had in his coat pocket, but I can tell you his threat got my attention. So I had a quick debate with myself. Was God calling me to stop preaching at this point and leave the ministry, or did He want me to continue and trust Him?

I remember whispering a prayer, "Lord, I don't know what that man has in his pocket. But I do know that every time I come out here to preach, I entrust myself to You. So I'm going to finish this message and if I perish, I perish."

At that moment, a new sense of security and power

welled up within me, and I preached harder than ever. I found new strength. It was almost as if the man threatening me had disappeared. And after a couple of minutes, he did disappear. He just walked away.

God can do that. He can remove people who would be destructive to you. He can protect His people.

Let me tell another true story that happened to a godly woman in our church in Dallas. She was being harassed and mistreated by her boss because she was a Christian, and he didn't like it because she wouldn't do some of the things the other people did.

This woman's boss made life miserable for her, and he regularly threatened to fire her. She came to see me and said, "I don't think I can take this anymore. I believe God wants me at this job, but my boss is abusing me. Please pray for me."

I asked this sister to fast. I encouraged her to use her dinnertime as a time of prayer when she laid her need before the Lord. She agreed to fast.

The next week, she was called into the office of her boss's supervisor, who informed her that her boss had been doing some inappropriate things at work and had just been fired. And she was being promoted to his position.

Someone may call that luck or coincidence. I call it fasting for God's protection and seeing His power at work.

Once Esther decided to fast, she told Mordecai and all the Jews to do the same. Esther 4:17 is an important verse: "So Mordecai went away and did just as Esther had commanded him."

Why is this verse significant? Because just a few verses earlier, Mordecai was telling her what to do. Now Esther was commanding Mordecai and everybody else to fast.

In other words, Esther had stopped being a fearful victim. She was no longer controlled by her fear. She was no longer victimized by Haman or her circumstances.

When you're a victim of fear, everybody else but God can tell you what to do. Your circumstances dictate your response. But when you tap into God's power by fasting, He steps in.

You can read the rest of the story on your own. You may already know how it ends. Esther arranged a private banquet with herself, the king, and Haman, at which she revealed Haman's plot and the fact that she and her people were going to be killed. Haman was condemned to death without even having the chance to speak in his own defense (Esther 7:1–10).

The bottom line is that Haman was hanged and the Jews were allowed to arm and defend themselves. On the day appointed for their slaughter, they routed their enemies and won a great victory.

When your life pleases God, He will make your enemies your footstool (see Psalm 110:1). When you fast and pray, you are appealing to a greater power, and God has the ability to rearrange circumstances. We have a powerful foe in Satan, but we serve the King of kings and Lord of lords. When we make our appeal to Him, it doesn't matter how powerful the enemy may be.

Several years ago, a man in Dallas threatened me

and my family because of our Christian stance. It was a very fearful time. We went home from church one day, and someone had dug up our lawn and thrown things around and created a mess.

Some other things happened that made it clear the Evans household needed protection. That was a disconcerting time, and I had to ask myself some hard questions about how much I really trusted God.

Fearful times like these will come in different forms for different people. They aren't always so dramatic, thank the Lord. But His protection is available in any circumstance. Fasting helps us activate God's power.

FASTING FOR MINISTRY

There's one more area of fasting I want to discuss because I have a passion and a burden to see every member of the body of Christ equipped for ministry, serving God with a sense of purpose and fulfillment.

I hope this describes your life and service for the Lord today, no matter what your occupation. But if you can't really say that you have discovered God's design for you, I want to show you how the discipline of fasting, accompanied by focused prayer, can help you find and follow His will for your personal ministry.

My concern is that too many Christians are not functioning the way God has designed them, called them, and gifted them to function. They seem to have no sense of divine appointment or spiritual destiny.

Some people think this kind of calling is limited to pastors, missionaries, and others in full-time Christian service who have a definite "job description." But every believer is called to serve Christ full-time. It may be that your occupation *is* your ministry, or it may facilitate your ministry. But either way, God wants you to live with a sense of divine destiny.

Before we get into this portion of our study on fasting, let me say that you have not really lived until you have found your God-given ministry. To live without a sense of divine appointment is to simply exist, to be detached from an eternal perspective and, therefore, simply marking time.

I liken the problem of being out of sync with your calling to the technique of falsetto in singing. I'm not an expert, or even a near-expert, when it comes to music. Everyone who knows me knows that I can't sing. But I know that falsetto is singing outside of your natural range.

The dictionary describes falsetto as "an artificially produced singing voice." Singing falsetto takes you above and beyond your natural voice, into a range that you can't sustain for very long without creating stress and strain on the vocal cords. Singers don't stay in falsetto. They go there and then come back to their normal range.

A lot of Christians attempt to serve Christ in falsetto. They are operating outside of their normal "range"— their calling and gifting from God. And just as a falsetto voice can be hard to sustain for a long period, it's hard to sustain your commitment and joy when you're straining.

How do you know if you're serving in falsetto? Answering these questions can help. In what ways is the kingdom of God benefiting from your service? Do you know what your calling is? Do you have a clear sense that God has His hand on your life for eternal purposes, or would you define your ministry in terms of your career aspirations only? Are you living out a kingdom agenda?

As we look into the Word to address these issues, let me show you a biblical example of serving in falsetto. As the church in Jerusalem grew, the apostles found themselves preaching and teaching while also being responsible to administer aid to the church's dependent widows (Acts 6:1). But some of the widows were being overlooked, and someone began to complain.

The apostles realized they were straining outside of their range to keep up with this important ministry. Their primary calling was not "to serve tables" (v. 2), but to the ministry of the Word and prayer.

So they called the congregation together and told them to select seven godly men to administer this service. These men did a magnificent job, the apostles were freed to fulfill their calling, and the church grew (vv. 3–7).

If you're searching for maximum effectiveness and joy in your Christian service, you need to know you're not the first Christian to do so. The apostles and other leaders in the early church had to search out God's will for their specific service.

In Acts 13:1–3, we find another example of the early church needing the Lord's guidance in ministry. One way those involved addressed this need was through fasting.

Acts 13:1 locates this story in the church at Antioch, a city in what is now Syria, about three hundred miles north of Jerusalem. The church there was blessed with some great leaders, including Barnabas and Paul, and became a strong missionary-sending church. These verses tell that story.

But for now, I want to go directly to verses 2–3, where we are told,

> While they [these leaders] were ministering to the Lord and fasting, the Holy Spirit said, "Set apart for Me Barnabas and Saul for the work to which I have called them." Then, when they had fasted and prayed and laid their hands on them, they sent them away.

You can see how intimately fasting is connected with the discovery of God's will and His appointment to ministry. Again, this is not just for apostles and prophets and pastors and missionaries. Let me give you four principles for the discipline of fasting for ministry, and help you use this powerful practice in your own life.

The Purpose of Fasting for Ministry

If you are confused or uncertain about what God would have you to do, one way to get clarity is through fasting and the focused prayer that should accompany it.

These leaders in the Antioch church knew God had something more for them, but they didn't know exactly what it was. But they were in the right place to receive that guidance, because they were coming before the Lord in fasting and prayer.

It's important to see that this guidance and commissioning for service came in the context of the
church. When you are fasting and seeking God for your
calling, don't expect Him to lead you and equip you
and send you out in total isolation from the rest of the
body of Christ. The church doesn't have any "Lone
Ranger" Christians.

The church is called to help believers discover their
ministry, equip them to handle it, and then provide
them with opportunities to carry out their calling. This
may be in the local body, or by commissioning and
sending out workers as we see here in Acts 13. You and
I need the church not simply as a place to worship God,
but as a place where we learn how to serve Him.

Service is at the heart of ministry. You have been
called and gifted to serve the Lord. Whatever you do for
people or with people, you are really doing for the Lord.
"It is the Lord Christ whom you serve," Paul wrote
(Colossians 3:24). He also said, "Whatever you do, do
all to the glory of God" (1 Corinthians 10:31).

These are some of the guidelines the Bible gives us
for determining our calling or ministry. The Word also
helps us determine the spiritual gift or gifts God has
given us.

Some people wish they could turn to the Bible and
find all the specifics for their lives. But God does something better than that. He provides us with spiritual
principles and guidelines we can apply in any situation.

The leaders at Antioch received their specific guidance when the Holy Spirit said, "Set apart for Me Barn-

abas and Saul" (Acts 13:2). The Spirit is God's "guidance counselor" for your ministry. The Spirit knows where to take you because He knows the mind of God and He knows your appointment.

We'll talk about the Holy Spirit's work of guidance in more detail later. For now, let's note that these men were fasting and seeking the Lord for the purpose of finding His direction in ministry.

The People Who Fast for Ministry

The second thing I want you to notice is that anybody and everybody in the church can practice fasting for ministry, because nobody in the church is excluded from ministry.

The leaders mentioned in Acts 13 were given to the church at Antioch to equip the believers there for ministry (see Ephesians 4:12). These leaders themselves illustrate the fact that nobody is excluded, because they were a multiracial, multicultural group in a church and a city that were multiracial and multicultural. God doesn't play favorites.

Barnabas was a Jew from Cyprus (Acts 4:36), a Gentile colony. He was a Grecian Jew, Jewish by birth but with a Gentile upbringing. This would be the same today as a white person who grew up in a black neighborhood, or a black person who grew up in a white neighborhood.

"Simeon who was called Niger" was another leader (Acts 13:1). *Niger* means black. Simeon was a black African exercising leadership at Antioch. The next man was Lucius of Cyrene, which was a North African country.

Then there was Manaen, "who had been brought up with Herod the tetrarch." Manaen represented royalty, the upper crust of society. Last, but by no means least, was Saul or Paul. He was the Jewish scholar, the local Pharisee. Paul was totally immersed in the Scriptures and Jewish culture.

The church at Antioch reflects the fact that God has a plan and a place of ministry for everyone. His desire is to reveal that plan to us, which is what happened as these leaders fasted and prayed.

The Praise of Fasting for Ministry

Acts 13:2 says that in addition to their fasting, these leaders were "ministering to the Lord." Prayer was certainly part of that ministry, and verse 3 mentions prayer specifically. This is where it starts getting rich!

To minister to the Lord is to get your praise going. To minister to the Lord is to be in His presence, so God-conscious and God-focused it's as if He is the only person in the room. In other words, praise should be an integral part of our fasting experience.

These men had laid aside food and were absorbed in worship and prayer when the answer came. "The Holy Spirit said, 'Set apart for Me Barnabas and Saul for the work to which I have called them.'"

Please notice the specificity of the Spirit's call. This was not vague direction or a general calling. When God calls a person to ministry, He calls that person individually and specifically. When you fast for direction in your ministry, God is able to provide that direction.

Barnabas and Saul were called to ministry, but it didn't happen until they were in God's presence. If you want to know God's will, you have to be in His presence. The more you're in His presence, the more specifically you'll hear His call.

I know what you may be thinking at this point. "Tony, that was great for Barnabas and Saul. But the Holy Spirit doesn't speak audibly like that today. How can I hear the Spirit's voice? How do I know when God is calling me?"

These are good questions, and I'd like to suggest that the answers are right here in Acts 13. It's time to go back to verse 1, where we learn that the leaders in the church at Antioch were "prophets and teachers." These ministries are key to our hearing the Spirit's voice today, because He speaks through the Word in the context of the church as the validating community of believers.

The Spirit can speak to you individually from any passage of Scripture.

I'll explain that in a minute, but first let's look at these two ministry functions. A prophet is someone who comes with a message from God and applies it to a specific situation. A prophet spoke with immediacy and with authority: "Thus saith the Lord." A prophet applied the Word right to the heart, no matter what the situation. That's why some prophets got themselves killed. People didn't want to hear what God was saying.

Since we have the full revelation of God today, He doesn't need to deliver a new message. The role of the prophet today is fulfilled when you go to church facing a particular need in your life and it seems the pastor prepared his sermon just for you. Or you're listening to the radio, and the speaker seems to be talking to you alone.

What happened is that the Holy Spirit applied the Word specifically to you. He can do that because He knows your personal need. The Spirit can speak to you individually from any passage of Scripture. So if you want to hear the Spirit's voice, you need to be in the Word and under the proclamation of the Word. This is another reason the church is so critically important.

The leaders at Antioch also included teachers. A teacher has a different function than a prophet. The ministry of teaching involves clearly communicating truth so that people understand what the Word is saying. A teacher helps you understand what the Bible means by what it says. The Spirit also speaks through teachers.

The Word is always primary, but there's a second way we can hear the Holy Spirit's voice in terms of guidance for ministry. His call on your life will be validated by others in the body of Christ.

You see, when the Holy Spirit called Barnabas and Saul for the church to send them out as missionaries, that call was validated by the other leaders—and, by extension, the entire church at Antioch. Their calling was verified by other spiritual people through whom God was speaking.

If God is telling you something through His Word, He's also going to validate it through other people. God won't call you to ministry contrary to the revelation of His Word. And if God is calling you, other godly people are going to recognize it.

Acts 15 gives a great example of this validation in the church council. God led the apostle James and the others to render a decision concerning the relationship between Jews and Gentiles in the church.

Then that decision was disseminated to the churches for validation, along with a letter that said in part, "It seemed good to the Holy Spirit and to us . . ." (v. 28). James and the council in Jerusalem wanted the churches to know that the Spirit had spoken and that His will had been recognized.

If you feel that God has a particular area of ministry for you, you can validate that call by submitting it to spiritual people in the church. The church is also key here because it provides the context in which ministry is carried out.

To bring it back full circle, let me say again that the beginning of the process was praise, worship, fasting, and prayer. If you want God to stir your heart in relation to ministry, or any direction in life, for that matter, get into His presence with other believers who are also seeking Him.

The Productivity of Fasting for Ministry

The result of the fasting and prayer in Acts 13:1–3 was the birth of world missions! Barnabas and Saul were sent out on the first-ever missionary trip sponsored by the church. The gospel was taken to the entire Roman Empire, the church grew, and Paul went on to write most of the New Testament. That's what I call productivity!

Let me tell you something about the calling God gives you. It will always be something bigger than what you could do on your own. If you can do it already without God, then it's not your calling. If you can pull it off without the power of prayer in total dependence upon God, it's not true ministry no matter what anybody calls it.

But when God calls you, it will be to a ministry that first teaches you how much you need Him, and then produces something significant for His kingdom. The measure of a ministry is its impact for the kingdom, revealing the glory of God so that the name of God is revered.

What impact are you making for the kingdom of God? What is it that you want God to do in your life, in your family, and in the church and community of which you are a part? What need are you facing for which you need God's help and intervention? No matter what your situation, I urge you and challenge you to take seriously the biblical discipline of fasting.

Our church in Dallas begins every year with a week of fasting and prayer for the individual, family, and corporate needs of our members. We have seen God do miracles in our church body as we give up food and television for spiritual breakthroughs. It is time for us to get our breakthrough from God.

A man was puzzled by the water that kept seeping into his basement. He would bail out the water and dry the basement, only to have the water return. He checked all the surface water connections and the drainage tiles around the basement, and everything was fine. He kept bailing water and drying the basement until he finally decided to call a plumber, who informed him that he had a leak under the house's foundation. The problem wasn't solved until the man broke up his basement floor, fixed the problem, and laid a new floor. Like this man, we spend time trying to bail and mop our way out of old problems, only to discover nothing much has changed.

We need to break up those old floors that are hiding the real problem and lay some new foundations. Fasting breaks up those old, hard floors in our hearts. So whether your need is power, deliverance from addictions, healing, help in your marriage, financial problems, guidance, revival, burdens, ministry, or any other situation too big for you to handle, get close to the Son through fasting and prayer.

THE URBAN ALTERNATIVE

The Philosophy

Dr. Tony Evans and TUA believe the answer to transforming our culture comes from the inside out and from the bottom up. We believe the core cause of the problems we face is a spiritual one; therefore, the only way to address them is spiritually. And that means the proclamation and application of biblical principles to the four areas of life—the individual, the family, the church, and the community. We've tried a political, social, economic, and even a religious agenda. It's time for a kingdom agenda.

The Purpose

We believe that when each biblical sphere of life functions properly, the net result is evangelism, discipleship, and community impact. As people learn how to govern themselves under God, they then transform the institutions of family, church, and government from a biblically based kingdom perspective.

The Programs

To achieve our goal we use a variety of strategies, methods, and resources for reaching and equipping as many people as possible.

- **Broadcast Media**
  The Urban Alternative reaches hundreds of thousands of people each day with a kingdom-based approach to life through its daily radio program, weekly television broadcast, and the Internet.

- **Leadership Training**
  Our national Church Development Conference, held annually, equips pastors and lay leaders to become agents of change. Teaching biblical methods of church ministry has helped congregations renew their sense of mission and expand their ministry impact.

- **Crusades/Conferences**
  Crusades are designed to bring churches together across racial, cultural, and denominational lines to win the lost. TUA also seeks to keep these churches together for ongoing fellowship and community impact. Conferences give Christians practical biblical insight on how to live victoriously in accordance with God's Word and His kingdom agenda in the four areas of life—personal, family, church, and community.

- **Resource Development**
  We are fostering lifelong learning partnerships with the people we serve by providing a variety of published materials. We offer books, audiotapes,

videos, and booklets to strengthen people in their walk with God and ministry to others.

- Project Turn-Around
  PTA is a comprehensive church-based community impact strategy. It addresses such areas as economic development, education, housing, health revitalization, family renewal and reconciliation. To model the success of the project, TUA invests in its own program locally. We also assist other churches in tailoring the model to meet the specific needs of their communities, while simultaneously addressing the spiritual and moral frame of reference.

* * *

For more information, a catalog of Dr. Tony Evans's ministry resources, and a complimentary copy of Dr. Evans's monthly devotional magazine,
call (800) 800-3222 or
write TUA at P.O. Box 4000, Dallas TX 75208.